LIMERATURE 101

LIMERATURE 101

LANCE HANSEN

HUMORIST BOOKS

New York

First Printing: 2023

ISBN 978-1-954158-25-2

Edited by Brian Boone

Layout by Marty Dundics

Humorist Books is an imprint of *Weekly Humorist* owned and operated by Humorist Media LLC.

Weekly Humorist is a weekly humor publication, subscribe online at weeklyhumorist.com

110 Wall Street New York, NY 10005

weeklyhumorist.com - humoristbooks.com - humoristmedia.com

For Rebecca and Dolly and Louisa

CLASS SYLLABUS

First Quarter: ANCIENT AND INFLUENTIAL VOICES

The Epic of Gilgamesh

The Aeneid

The Odyssey

Argonautica

Beowulf

The Divine Comedy

Macbeth

Paradise Lost

The Tyger

Pride and Prejudice

The Scarlet Letter

Oliver Twist

Jane Eyre

Moby-Dick

Second Quarter: TITANS OF GLOBAL LITERATURE

The Picture of Dorian Gray

Crime and Punishment

The Metamorphosis

Ulysses

Brave New World

The Stranger

No Exit

Waiting for Godot

Nineteen Eighty-Four

The Lord of the Flies

Lolita

Things Fall Apart

Prick Up Your Ears

The Unbearable Lightness of Being

Third Quarter: AMERICAN REVOLUTIONARIES

The Adventures of Huckleberry Finn

The Call of the Wild

The Great Gatsby

The Sun Also Rises

As I Lay Dying

Tropic of Cancer

They Shoot Horses, Don't They?

Gone With the Wind

Of Mice and Men

Their Eyes Were Watching God

A Streetcar Named Desire

Death of a Salesman

The Catcher in the Rye

A Good Man is Hard to Find

Giovanni's Room

On the Road

Naked Lunch

Catch-22

Fourth Quarter: MODERNISTS AND POPULISTS

The Postman Always Rings Twice

The Crying of Lot 49

Where Are You Going, Where Have You Been?

A&P

The Lottery

The Naked and the Dead

The Fountainhead

Who's Afraid of Virginia Woolf?

Slaughterhouse-Five

Carrie

Factotum

SUPPLEMENTAL MATERIALS

Welcome to LIMERATURE 101

"Between 2012 and 2019, the number of bachelor's degrees awarded annually in English fell by twenty-six percent, in philosophy and religious studies by twenty-five percent, and in foreign languages and literature by twenty-four percent."
—Louis Menand, "What's So Great About Great-Books Courses?", *The New Yorker, 2021*

In a bid to remedy this development, several institutions have adjusted their course structure to significantly reduce the workload. This trend is reflected in the latest addition to the Core Curriculum of a nearby college, where as a means of lightening the burden on today's busy student, all literature has been condensed.

First Quarter: ANCIENT AND INFLUENTIAL VOICES

The Epic of Gilgamesh

When the Gods made his buddy get sick
This king lost his feral sidekick
In an existential crisis
He abandoned his vices
And became somewhat less of a prick

(author image unavailable)

Aeneid

Aeneas: Rome's golden boy
Told Ulysses they needed a ploy
So they hid (rather reckless)
In a big wooden equus
And popped out once they got into Troy

Virgil

The Odyssey

Hero of Trojan War fame
Had only himself to blame
Don't get strung out on lotus;
Sirens' call? Don't take notice;
And don't EVER give cyclops your name

Homer

Argonautica

Jason, that sailor from Greece
Was sent off to look for a fleece.
He then, for a bargain, gots
Fifty-some Argonauts
And the Lemnian girls all got a piece

Apollonius of Rhodes

Beowulf

This fellow's heroic quest
Was seeking out beasts he could best:
One who'd leveled a tavern,
Then its mom, in a cavern,
Then a dragon — materially obsessed

(author image unavailable)

The Divine Comedy

Virgil and Dante went off hand in hand
To take in the sights where souls go
when they're damned
Come to find Hell's a scorcher
(With ironical torture)
Meanwhile, Limbo and Heaven are bland

Dante Alighieri

Macbeth

Weird sisters while stirring their pot
Set in motion an unsav'ry plot
Soon the king, wracked with guilt
Feels a chill up his kilt
As his wife tries to rub out a spot

William Shakespeare

Paradise Lost

Adam was tough to convince
Into taking a bite of that quince.
Turns out his undoing
Was the girl he was wooing
And the Garden has been vacant since

John Milton

The Tyger

In its day this short poem was felt
To be scand'lous, since mostly it dealt
With God's knack for creatin'
Them who eat and get ate-in'
(Not to mention, the title's misspelt!!)

William Blake

Pride and Prejudice

When first they met, Darcy dismissed her
When Lizzie rebuked him, he missed her
A courtship of quarrels
But surely the moral's:
"Keep Wickham away from your sister!"

Jane Austen

The Scarlet Letter

A pregnant young lady named Prynne
Was condemned for committing this sin
Her husband, disguised,
Returned and surmised:
"Is the pastor this kid's next of kin?!?"

Nathaniel Hawthorne

Oliver Twist

The tale of a street urchin who
Falls into the seedy milieu
Of a waif — name of Dodger,
A felonious codger,
And their larcenous underage crew

Charles Dickens

Jane Eyre

Young girl meets a man from the Moors
Whose wife crawls around on all fours
When this crazed, feral spouse
Burns herself and the house
The girl gets the man she adores

Charlotte Brontë

Moby-Dick

A peg-legged salt from Nantucket
Aboard the Pequod — a rusty ol' bucket
Nailed up a doubloon
Grabbed his trusty harpoon
And like caution, decided to chuck it

Herman Melville

Second Quarter: TITANS OF GLOBAL LITERATURE

The Picture of Dorian Gray

Hedonistic and handsome young Brit
All this time and he's not aged a bit.
Despite years of depravity,
He's somehow defied gravity
But that portrait of him looks like SHIT!

Oscar Wilde

Crime and Punishment

Ex-student plots and attacks
Some greedy old broad with an axe
He finally confesses
(Turns out he possesses
The morals he wishes he lacks)

Fyodor Dostoevsky

The Metamorphosis

A traveling salesman named Gregor
Awoke as a gruesome six-legger
He was finally finished
By a young violinist:
"Bug-Boy won't make ME a beggar!"

Franz Kafka

Ulysses

Here is Bloom, the Odysseus of Dublin
His intestines and consciousness bubblin'
Seems the streams he would spew
While he's crouched in the loo
Were the ones critics found the most troublin'

James Joyce

Brave New World

A misfitted twerp Alpha Plus
Views status with deep-held distrust.
Soon a strange, savage bastard
(Who's got Shakespeare mastered!!)
Becomes his "in" with the elite upper-crust

Aldous Huxley

The Stranger

A young man who can't empathize
Who's unmoved by his mother's demise,
Fills an Arab with slugs
And responds with more shrugs,
And he doesn't care much if he dies.

Albert Camus

No Exit

Garcin, Inez, and Estelle
Three souls sharing one room in hell
Garcin half jokes:
"Hell is other folks"
And the Valet don't answer the bell

Jean-Paul Sartre

Waiting for Godot

Beneath a bald willow, two mopes
Begin to abandon their hopes.
A couple leaves grow,
The guy's a no-show.
Day three, they'll return with some ropes.

Samuel Beckett

Nineteen Eighty-Four

As one of the State's bureaucrats
Winston Smith's job was doctoring stats
Then he sold out his lover,
Pledged his heart to Big Brother
To avoid being eaten by rats

George Orwell

The Lord of the Flies

The children split up into cliques
Got naked and sharpened their sticks
Soon these war painted kids
Really let loose their ids
-Just your typical day's politics

William Golding

Lolita

Humbert Humbert, erudite gent
Penned memoirs behind Portland Cement.
He'd married a blighter,
And murdered a writer,
And did worse to the age of consent!

Vladimir Nabokov

Things Fall Apart

A wrestler, afraid of disgrace
Kills a kid in the hopes to save face
Since the death of the child
Things get bad (he's exiled)
Comes back home to find whites run the place!

Chinua Achebe

Prick Up Your Ears

True tale of a playwright named Orton
Well-known for libid'nous consortin'
Throughout London's latrines
'Till his lover, it seems,
Used a hammer to end Joe's cavortin'

John Lahr

The Unbearable Lightness of Being

A handsome young surgeon from Prague
Adrift in a philanderous fog
Between a girl in a bowler
And his wife, a bipolar
Who spends most of her time with a dog

Milan Kundera

Third Quarter: AMERICAN REVOLUTIONARIES

The Adventures of Huckleberry Finn

Having faked his own death, a young knave
Sets adrift with a runaway slave
On this picaresque quest he
Meets up with his bestie
(A boy who's not wont to behave)

Mark Twain

The Call of the Wild

A spoiled St. Bernard (sans barrel)
Is thrust into a life of great peril
After leaving behind
All ties to mankind
He figures he's better off feral

Jack London

The Great Gatsby

Despite elegant clothes, gloves, and spats
You can't blend with true aristocrats.
Ditch your lavish soirée,
Douse the light 'cross the bay;
Shoulda quit while your name was still Gatz.

F. Scott Fitzgerald

The Sun Also Rises

Jake, an impotent scribe
Travels with his bohemian tribe
And a hip divorcé
(Who's a matador's bae)
-Cue the fisticuffs once they imbibe.

Ernest Hemingway

As I Lay Dying

The Bundren kids and their daddy
Pack up their expired mother Addie
And haul the stiff off in
A hast'ly made coffin
Then roll into town smelling badly

William Faulkner

Tropic of Cancer

The author, at just over thirty
Was debauched, perverse, squalid, and wordy
And his roman à clef
Don't have much in the way
Of a structure, but BOY is it dirty!

Henry Miller

They Shoot Horses, Don't They?

A failed ingenue name of Gloria
To her dance partner: "Not just to worry ya"
(Pulls a gun from her purse)
"After hoofing- and worse"
"I've come down with a touch of dysphoria."

Horace McCoy

Gone with the Wind

This greatest of peniaphobes
Sees her life start to turn out like Job's
When the South started hurtin'
Stitched a dress from a curtain
From a sheet she made Rhett's hooded robes

Margaret Mitchell

Of Mice and Men

A man-child, with rather odd habits
Of picking up ducks, mice, and rabbits
And wringing their necks,
Is mistook for a sex-
Fiend by folks in the town he inhabits.

John Steinbeck

Their Eyes Were Watching God

Dismayed with the men she had picked
This widow found someone who clicked
But she killed her mad suitor
Who attempted to shoot her
And the jury chose not to convict

Zora Neale Hurston

A Streetcar Named Desire

New transplant to the French Quarter,
Blanche DuBois is an uneasy boarder
Of her kid sister Stella,
Whose gruff, brutish fellah
Takes advantage of Blanche's disorder.

Tennessee Williams

Death of a Salesman

A rep who has just had a vision
Makes a dotage-inspired decision
Worth more dead than alive,
He sets out for a drive
Seeking payouts for life AND collision

Arthur Miller

The Catcher in the Rye

Depressed prep school dropout, revealed
Using misanthropy as a shield
With his comments satiric
And a misconstrued lyric
About kids falling down in a field

J.D. Salinger

A Good Man is Hard to Find

Old lady on a trip with the fam
Encounters three men on the lam
Once the convicts get rid
Of the folks and each kid
Their leader makes chit-chat with gram

Flannery O'Connor

Giovanni's Room

While in France, contemplating a wedding,
David meets the paison he starts bedding.
He expresses much doubt
When he's pressed to come out
Then feels guilt 'bout his lover's beheading

James Baldwin

On the Road

Struggling writer named Sal
Follows freewheeling, ex-convict pal
Name of Dean Moriarty
(The life of the party),
From locale to locale to locale...

Jack Kerouac

Naked Lunch

A junkie in search of a fix
Finds he's caught himself up in a mix
With all manner of bugs,
Orgies, sadists, and drugs
Which secrete from some humanoids' dix.

William S. Burroughs

Catch-22

A sardonic, young bombardier
Hopes to wrap up his army career.
But a rule (paradoxic)
Makes his struggle quixotic,
While enriching the war profiteer.

Joseph Heller

Fourth Quarter: MODERNISTS AND POPULISTS

The Postman Always Rings Twice

A cad with a penchant to drift
Gets caught up in a murderous grift
With an unfaithful broad
And a scheme to defraud
And naturally, justice is swift

James M. Cain

The Crying of Lot 49

With increased paranoic anxiety
Mrs. Maas starts to spot a variety
Of odd little doodles —
Crude post carriers' bugles —
Do they hint at some secret society?!?

Thomas Pynchon

Where Are You Going? Where Have You Been?

Mysterious creep Arnold Friend
Pulled his golden car right 'round the bend
Cryptic scrawls on the Caddy
And the threats to her daddy
Lead to Connie's ambiguous end

Joyce Carol Oates

A&P

The teen clerk can't help himself staring
As three girls go shopping for herring
All clad in bikini
The first, he dubs "Queenie"
Quits his job, but finds nobody's caring

John Updike

The Lottery

The lists are writ up through the dawn
As the town square attracts lookers-on
Each house gets a box
The kids gather rocks
And then one lucky winner is drawn!

Shirley Jackson

The Naked and the Dead

The new recruit panics and shits
Before getting himself blown to bits
Which gives the platoon
A prolonged sense of doom
'Till the Japanese force up and quits

Norman Mailer

The Fountainhead

Square-jawed young architect Howard
Looked up as his masterpiece towered
After throwing some fits
Blew the fucker to bits
Once his feelings about it had soured

Ayn Rand

Who's Afraid of Virginia Woolf?

A couple-unhappily spoused
And some newlyweds, get themselves soused.
Seems these two drunken louts
Have belligerent bouts
Since their hope for a child has been doused

Edward Albee

Slaughterhouse-Five

A time-traveling prisoner of war
Hiding out in an old abattoir
Finds himself whisked off to
Some strange alien zoo
Making love to a missing porn star.

Kurt Vonnegut

Carrie

The newly crowned prom queen glowers,
Before showing classmates her powers.
In the gym she unleashes
Her telekinesis.
Don't toss tampons at girls in the showers!

Stephen King

Factotum

A down and out bard — rather boozy
Lacks a publisher (he's a bit choosey)
He loses some gigs
(And the lady he digs)
Then hooks up with a gold-digging floozy

Charles Bukowski

The World According to Garp

Sweet story 'bout a nurse and her son,
And some ladies who lop off their tongues.
There's rape, assassination,
Some literal castration,
And a bear, of course, thrown in for fun!

John Irving

A Confederacy of Dunces

Mother Reilly, her son's sole defender
While lit, had a small fender-bender.
So, her son — learned slob
Had to take on a job
As a pirate-costumed hot dog vendor

John Kennedy Toole

Love in the Time of Cholera

She dumped him, just like her dad said
Met a surgeon and got herself wed
Despite all his trysts,
Florentino's int'rysts
Were piqued when the doctor dropped dead

Gabriel García Márquez

The Bonfire of the Vanities

Wall Streeter Sherman McCoy
And his mistress run over a boy.
Then the press and the system
Toss, tug him, and twist him:
Like a Master of the Universe toy

Tom Wolfe

The Joy Luck Club

The tribulations and trials
Spanning ages and cultures and miles
All the worries and qualms
Between daughters and moms
Are discussed over their mahjong tiles

Amy Tan

The Firm

Ambitious young Ivy League grad
Lands a great job with perks (car and pad!)
But suspects his employers
Have rubbed out some lawyers
Who says that all mobsters are bad?

John Grisham

Infinite Jest

Master reel of obscure celluloid,
Renders viewers completely devoid
Of any shit-giving,
Or purpose for living**

**with copious footnotes employed

David Foster Wallace

American Tabloid

Three lawman, jaded and callous
Each busily meas'ring his phallus
Get in over their heads
(Castro, Mob, and the feds!!)
While conspiring in '63 Dallas

James Ellroy

Into the Wild

Adventuresome, outdoorsy scamp;
Starts to call himself Al Supertramp;
With this new nomenclature,
He sets off, back to nature;
Now kids snap selfies outside his camp.

Jon Krakauer

The Da Vinci Code

When a murder quite swiftly befalls
A curator while dressing the walls
A professor of symbols
Finds Macys and Gimbels
Ain't got SHIT on a couple cabals

Dan Brown

Gone Girl

By all accounts blissfully wed
'Till she disappears (presumed dead)
A fraudulent diary
Leads police to inquiry
But is she messing with everyone's head?

Gillian Flynn

SUPPLEMENTAL MATERIALS

The Limerick

A Professor must ramble and roam
To compile a such scholarly tome
And this field is quite sparse —
Highbrow volumes, which parse
And dissect each scat'logical pome

Gershon Legman

ACKNOWLEDGMENTS

The author would like to acknowledge the following people for their valuable input regarding this project: Patricia Barker, Brian Boone, Aarron Coleman, Marty Dundics, Micky Clement, Michael Gerber, Kelly Hansen, Tommy Hansen, Kit Lively, Courtney Mendenhall, Carl and Julie Muehleisen, Brian O'Brian, E.J. O'Hara, Michael Pershan, Scott Smith, Rich Sparks, Steve Teare and Joe Ziegler.

Special thanks to my high school English teachers, Mrs. Stevenson, Mrs. Sylvester and, especially, Mrs. Crumpton, who taught the 9th grade class, "Problems of Modern Man", where we read a number of these books.

About the Instructor

A desperate writer named Lance
Sought to pare novels down to a glance
The unmoved literati
Took one look at his body
Of work and declared, "Not a chance."

Made in the USA
Middletown, DE
16 October 2023

40938802R00091